BABY STEPS

To Grandma and Harlmoni

BABY STEPS

written and illustrated by

Peter McCarty

Henry Holt and Company

New York

This is baby Suki.
She is one day old.
The nurse wraps her tightly in a blanket.
We call her our little burrito.

Resting in her mother's arms,
Suki is one month old.
She is warm and happy,
and for the moment she is quiet.

Suki insists on being held in the air.
She is two months old.
With her fat cheeks and pink pajamas,
she looks like a flying piglet.

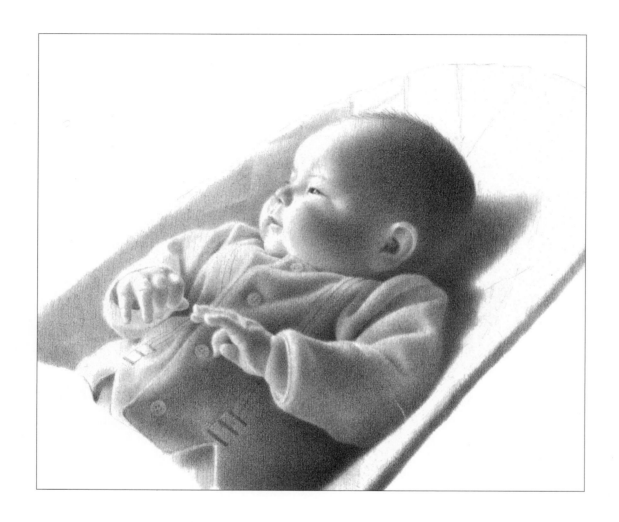

Sitting quietly in her bouncy chair,
Suki is three months old.

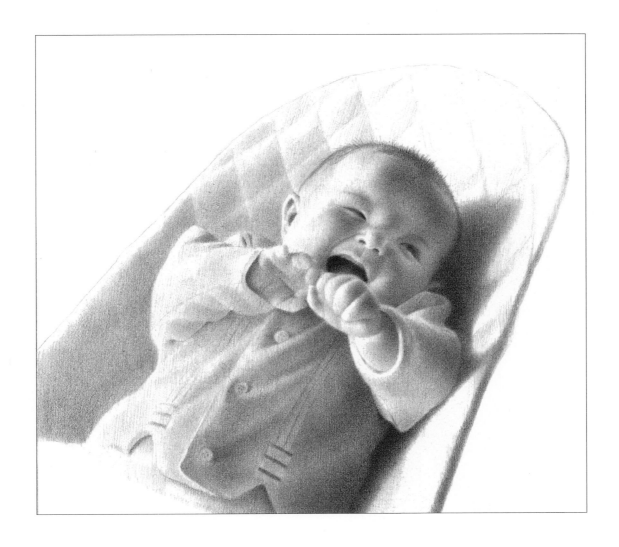

When she is happy, she puts her hands together
and squeals with delight.

The weather is getting warmer.
Suki is four months old.
Her mother carries her outside,
where Suki kicks her feet and smiles.

Suki feeds herself a cracker.
She is five months old.
She has favorite foods now,
like cereal and pears.

On a bright spring day,
Suki is six months old.
She lies in the grass
watching bees and butterflies.

Sitting on her own,
Suki is seven months old.
She reaches for her mobile.
She loves the way it moves.

On a hot summer's day,
Suki is eight months old.
She takes a nap at ten o'clock
and then again at two.

Suki takes her first trip to the beach.
She is nine months old.
With her mother beside her,
she plays at the water's edge.

Suki stands up tall.
She is ten months old.
In this month of milestones,
she crawls, talks, and bounces to music.

Suki flips through her book.
She is eleven months old.
She says lots of words,
but her favorite one is *button*.

Today is Suki's birthday.
She is one year old.
To celebrate,
she wears a very special dress.

Happy birthday, Suki!

Suki takes her first steps.
She is a big girl now.

Go, Suki, go!

Henry Holt and Company, LLC
Publishers since 1866
115 West 18th Street
New York, New York 10011

Henry Holt is a registered trademark of Henry Holt and Company, LLC
Copyright © 2000 by Peter McCarty
All rights reserved.
Published in Canada by Fitzhenry & Whiteside Ltd., 195 Allstate Parkway, Markham, Ontario L3R 4T8.

Library of Congress Cataloging-in-Publication Data
McCarty, Peter.
Baby steps / written and illustrated by Peter McCarty.
Summary: Baby Suki grows from one day old to one year old, squealing, smiling,
eating, reaching for her mobile, taking naps, and playing.
[1. Babies—Fiction. 2. Growth—Fiction.]   I. Title.
PZ7.M12835 Su 2000 [E]—dc21   99-46685

ISBN 0-8050-5953-9 / First Edition—2000
The artist used pencil on watercolor paper to create the illustrations for this book.
Designed by Martha Rago
Printed in the United States of America on acid-free paper. ∞
1   3   5   7   9   10   8   6   4   2